Savvy

Glam and Gorgeous ROOM

DIY PROJECTS FOR A STYLISH ROOM

by

Heather Wutschke

CAPSTONE PRESS
a capstone imprint

Savvy Books are published by Capstone Press,
1710 Roe Crest Drive, North Mankato, Minnesota 56003
www.mycapstone.com

Library of Congress Cataloging-in-Publication Data is available on the
Library of Congress website.
ISBN: 978-1-5157-4009-4 (hardcover)
ISBN: 978-1-5157-4012-4 (eBook PDF)

Summary: A craft and project book to help redecorate, organize,
and make a bedroom more glamorous and reflect personal style.

Editor: Kristen Mohn
Designer: Lori Bye
Creative Director: Heather Kindseth

Projects crafted by:
Heather Wutschke, Lori Bye, Shelli Frana, Amy Trina,
Karon Dubke, Marcy Morin, and Sarah Schuette

Image credits:
All photographs by Capstone Studio/Karon Dubke, Heather Kindseth except:
Shutterstock: Analgin, design element throughout, Artnis, design elements throughout,
ConstantinosZ, (purple sneakers) 29, Godsend, (watercolors) Cover, 1, Heiko Kueverling, 3, 28, 29,
indigolotos, (black shoe boxes) 29, IndiPixi, design element throughout,
IreneArt, design element throughout, kbecca, design element throughout

Printed and bound in Canada.
010395F17

Table of Contents

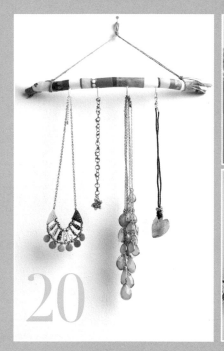

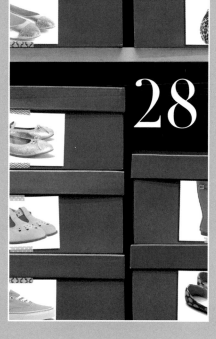

Make Your Room
GLAM & GORGEOUS!

Let your personal space reflect your glamorous side! This is your chance to revamp your room from top to bottom with simple tools and steps. Fab furniture remakes and display-worthy organization solutions can turn an average room into a gorgeous sanctuary just for you.

This project guide is designed to help you develop your own personal style and make your room into a more beautiful, more functional space that celebrates you. ROOM LOVE will help you achieve high style on any budget with upcycled, recycled, or made-from-scratch projects and crafts that you can do yourself. Each one is designed to show off your unique style. Happy DIY! And remember:

Everything in your room should bring you joy!

Outfit
PLANNER

Instead of rolling out of bed each morning and staring at your closet when you're half asleep, choose your outfits in advance. On weekends, look at your week ahead and decide what to wear each day. Monday mornings will be a breeze!

Supplies

Polaroid or any camera
   and printer

step stool

newspapers

12 x 9-inch canvas

acrylic paint (variety of colors)

large paintbrush

5 clothespins

small paintbrush

cardboard

scissors

tape

washi tape

gold pen

hot glue gun and glue

Steps

1. Take pictures of your favorite outfits, arranging your tops, bottoms, shoes, and accessories. Use the floor or a light-colored surface as a backdrop. Shoot pictures from overhead, standing on a stool if you need extra height. Print photos.

2. Put newspapers down on your work surface. Paint your canvas using large brush. Allow to dry.

3. Paint your clothespins using small brush. Allow to dry.

4. Use cardboard, scissors, and tape to make 2 small boxes to hold your photos. Make boxes short enough to allow tops of photos to show. Cover your boxes with washi tape.

5. Use gold pen to label your clothespins for each weekday, Monday through Friday.

6. Position boxes and clothespins on canvas with sample photos in place to determine how to space them. Then glue both boxes to the top of your canvas and each clothespin to the bottom of your canvas.

7. Use gold pen to make labels to categorize boxes for seasons or weather.

8. Plan your outfits for the following week by placing one on each clothespin. Add remaining photos to your boxes.

Dresser
MAKEOVER

This project is a great hand-me-down furniture solution!
Take something outdated or boring and turn it into something
beautiful and unique.

8

Supplies

dresser or any piece of furniture
   you want to stencil
drop cloth
medium-grade sandpaper
slightly damp paper towels
paint with primer for base color (satin finish)
paint tray
paintbrush
stencil
painter's tape
acrylic paint for stencil
stencil brush

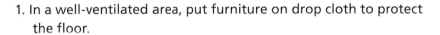

Steps

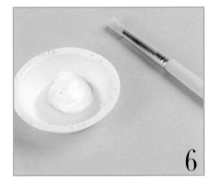

6

7

1. In a well-ventilated area, put furniture on drop cloth to protect the floor.

2. Sand furniture if you are going to paint it before stenciling.

3. After sanding, wipe the surface down with damp paper towels. Allow to dry.

4. Apply two coats of paint, letting it dry between coats. Let dry overnight before stenciling.

5. Plan out stencil design and position first stencil where you want it on furniture, adhering it with painter's tape so it doesn't shift.

6. Dip stencil brush in stencil paint and gently press down directly onto the stencil. Remove stencil and rinse and dry it while the paint is still wet.

7. Place stencil in the next place you want it and repeat process until you have the design you like.

Tip

Don't overload your stencil brush with paint or it will seep under the stencil edges.

9

Drawer DIVIDERS

Have all your drawers become junk drawers because you throw whatever you find into them? Put old boxes to work and give every drawer order and purpose with these cost-nothing, style-boosting dividers. Use different-size boxes depending on what goes in each drawer — smaller boxes for craft supplies or hair supplies, larger boxes for socks and underwear.

Supplies

tape measure or ruler
cereal or other boxes
scissors
contact paper

Steps

1. Cut the top and bottom off of each box to get two dividers from each. Cut them short enough to fit inside the drawer and allow it to close easily.

2. Arrange boxes in drawer to see how they fit best.

3. Put a sheet of contact paper pattern-side down on workspace. (Do not remove the backing yet.) Set first box on the contact paper.

4. Cut the paper so it will wrap over the sides to cover the inner and outer sides of the box.

5. Now remove backing from contact paper. Fold up the sides and stick the paper to the box.

6. Measure inside bottom of box. Cut contact paper to fit. Remove backing and stick to inside bottom of box.

7. Repeat until each box is covered. Place boxes in the drawer and organize your things!

Gold-Accented FURNITURE

Dip-dyed legs of tables or chairs can make a huge impact in your room. It's a super simple way to add sophistication to your space. Use gold, silver, or any color you want to create a personalized look. Turn old, hand-me-down furniture into something you love!

Supplies

chair or table

medium-grade sandpaper

slightly damp paper towels

drop cloth

spray paint

tape measure or ruler

pencil

painter's tape

gold acrylic paint

small paintbrush

Steps

If you're just adding gold tips, you can skip to step 4.

1. Put down drop cloth in well-ventilated area. Sand furniture.

2. Wipe down with damp paper towels. Allow to dry.

3. Paint table with 2–3 light coats of spray paint, allowing it to dry between coats. Let dry overnight.

4. Turn furniture upside down. Measure 5–10 inches from the end of each leg, depending on how much accent you want. Mark with a pencil. Apply painter's tape around legs below pencil line for a clean edge.

5. Apply three coats of gold acrylic paint with paintbrush.

6. Allow paint to dry and then remove painter's tape.

Washi Tape
MAKEOVER

Use this colorful adhesive to revamp just about any item in your room. It's quick and cheap — and easy to change up if next week you decide you're mad for polka dots instead of stripes! If you want the surface to become more permanent, you can add a decoupage sealer.

Supplies

furniture

slightly damp paper towel

washi tape

scissors

tape measure or ruler

pencil

Steps

1. Wipe surface with paper towel and let dry.

2. Plan your design. Create a pattern or just do a washi trim around the edges.

3. Tape away! Use a ruler or tape measure if you are worried about crooked lines. Measure and lightly mark with a pencil on each end of the table to guide the washi tape.

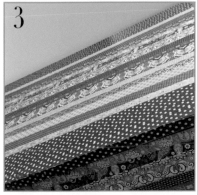

Tip

You can store things in the oatmeal container. This will also help to weigh it down so it won't tip over easily.

Hair Accessory
HOLDER

Headbands are easy to wear, stylish, and can save you if you only have a second to do your hair before you rush off to school. This funky display shows off your headwear and keeps it handy so you can grab, style, and go!

Supplies

pillar candle holder

acrylic paint

small paintbrush

2 12 x 12-inch sheets of
    scrapbook paper

scissors

tape measure

empty 42 oz. oatmeal
    container (large size)

decoupage glue

brush for decoupage

plastic scraper or plastic card

hot glue gun and glue

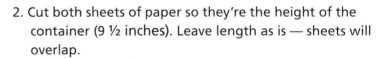

Steps

1. Paint pillar and allow to dry.

2. Cut both sheets of paper so they're the height of the container (9 ½ inches). Leave length as is — sheets will overlap.

3. Spread decoupage on sides of container. Line up the short side of one sheet of paper with the height of container. Wrap it around and smooth out with scraper. Put on second sheet of paper to cover rest of container. You'll need to apply another layer of decoupage where the sheets overlap. Smooth with scraper.

4. Spread more decoupage over the top of both sheets of paper. Allow to dry.

5. Use hot glue gun to adhere oatmeal container to the pillar. Put on the lid.

6. Put headbands around container and fill the container with hair supplies!

Tip

Make sure the fabric is porous enough for earrings to hook and remove without snagging.

Easy Peasy
EARRING HOLDER

If all your earrings are jumbled together in a box, separated from their partners, reunite them and show them off with this clever DIY display. Add it to a photo collage with other frames on your wall and it becomes a work of art!

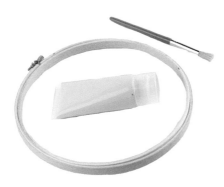

Supplies

embroidery hoop

acrylic paint

paintbrush

fabric (thin works best)

scissors

Steps

1. Remove screw from the top of the embroidery hoop so the two wood pieces come apart. Paint each piece and let dry.

2. Place the smaller hoop on a flat surface.

3. Lay the fabric pattern-side up over this hoop.

4. Place the larger hoop over the fabric. Press down so the small hoop comes up through the large hoop and fits together.

5. Replace screw and tighten. This will hold the fabric in place.

6. Trim excess fabric from the back of the hoop.

7. Poke your earrings through the fabric. For earrings with backs, you can place those on the earring posts from the back side of the fabric.

Driftwood
JEWELRY HANGER

Don't hide your jewelry in a box — make it into DIY wall art! Display your favorite pieces and show your artistic skill by painting a piece of driftwood in coordinating colors and patterns.

Supplies

large piece of driftwood

acrylic paint

paintbrush

painter's tape

4–6 craft hooks

string or ribbon

scissors

nail or tack

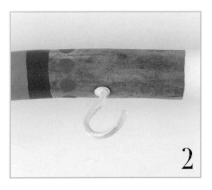

Steps

1. Pick a color palette and paint a design on the driftwood. Use painter's tape to paint clean stripes. Allow to dry.

2. Gently press hooks into bottom of the stick, screwing them in. Make sure hooks are pointing forward when done.

3. Cut string or ribbon and tie to each end.

4. Display favorites necklaces or bracelets on the hooks. Ask a parent if you can nail it on your wall, or hang it from a tackboard.

Sunglasses
HOLDER

No one likes a pair of scratched sunglasses, right? Here's a great way to store and show off your fabulous shades. Quick and easy — and it makes artwork out of your eyewear!

Supplies

11 x 14-inch picture frame
ice pick or thumbtack
4 screw eyes
wire

Steps

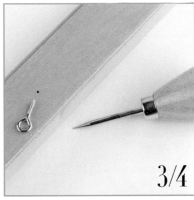

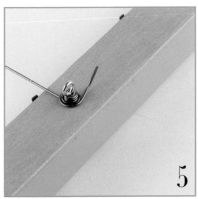

1. Remove backing and glass from frame. Be very careful when removing glass as edges will be sharp.

2. Lay frame flat on floor. Arrange sunglasses in frame to determine where you would like the two rows to be.

3. Flip the frame over. Use the ice pick or thumbtack to create holes on each side where you want the wires to attach.

4. Insert a screw eye into each hole.

5. Wrap wire through and around one screw a few times to secure. Pull wire tight to the other side of the frame. Wrap wire onto the opposite screw. Repeat for second row.

6. Set frame in the window or ask if you can nail it to your wall.

Magnetic
MAKEUP BOARD

Declutter your drawers and dresser tops and create easy access to lip balms, lotions, deodorant, and other things you use every day by magnetizing them! Frame all your essentials for a fun and clever boutique display.

Supplies

12 x 12-inch picture frame
butter knife
12 x 12-inch sheet metal
hot glue gun and glue
small magnets

Steps

1. If the frame has tabs on the back, use butter knife to lift them and carefully remove the glass. Glass edges will be sharp.

2. Replace glass with sheet metal and resecure back of frame.

3. Find makeup or other items you want to keep handy.

4. Glue a magnet onto back of each item.

5. Organize items onto sheet metal. Your morning routine will be a snap!

Washi Tape
HANGERS

Add some style and organization to your closet with these pretty hangers. Shower curtain hooks are a cheap, space-saving solution to consolidate hats and tank tops onto one hanger.

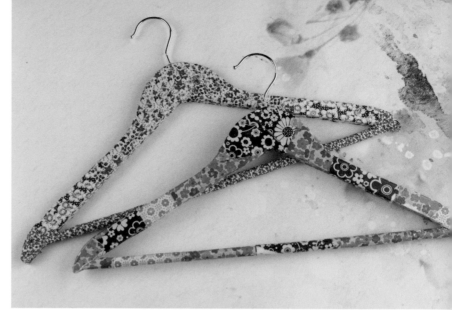

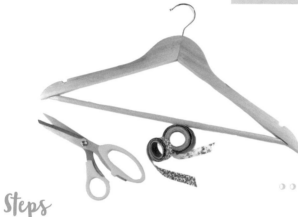

Supplies

wooden hangers
fabric washi tape
scissors
shower curtain rings

Steps

1. Start near the hook and wrap washi tape around the wooden part of the hanger, working toward the end. You can wrap straight from the roll or cut tape into strips and wrap one at a time. Continue wrapping until you have covered the entire wooden portion.

2. For organizing tank tops and hats, hang shower curtain rings on the bottom of the hanger and hook items to the rings. For scarves, simply tie them onto the hanger.

Yarn Bomb
HANGERS

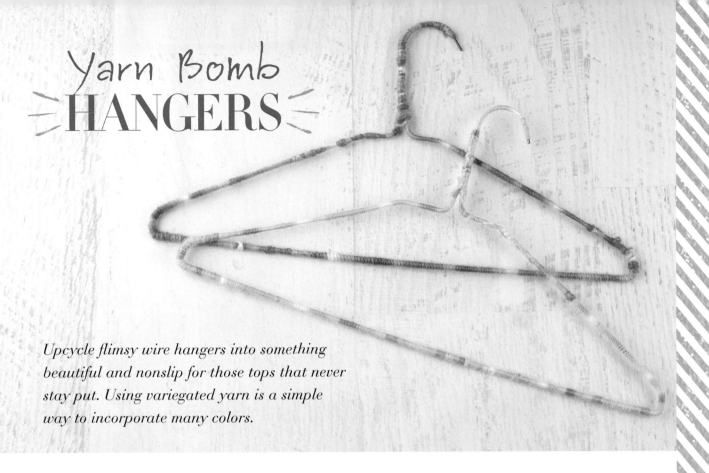

Upcycle flimsy wire hangers into something beautiful and nonslip for those tops that never stay put. Using variegated yarn is a simple way to incorporate many colors.

Tip
To make the hanger thicker, stack 2–3 hangers together before wrapping with yarn.

Supplies

wire hangers
yarn
scissors
hot glue gun and glue

Steps

1. Tie yarn to the neck of the hanger

2. Tightly wrap yarn around the hanger. As you wrap, use a dab of glue every now and then to keep yarn in place.

3. Wrap the yarn tightly to cover the entire hanger. Once fully covered, snip the end and glue to secure in place.

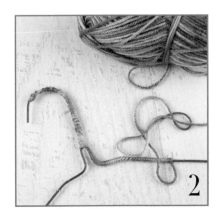

27

Boutique Shoe
ORGANIZING

No more digging for your left ballet flat in a messy shoe pile! Here is a simple, upcycled way to organize your shoe collection and keep stock of what you have. Add a cute bench nearby so you can sit and slip on your Cinderella slippers before dashing out the door.

Supplies

newspapers

shoe boxes

spray paint

camera and printer

washi tape

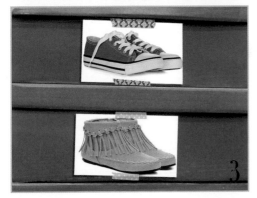

Steps

1. In a well-ventilated area, prepare work area by laying out newspapers. Spray paint each shoe box and lid. Allow to dry.

2. Snap a photo of each pair of shoes. Print photos.

3. Place shoes in boxes and attach matching photo to the end of each box with washi tape.

4. Stack boxes neatly or place on a shelf for easy access!

Rose
WALL CLOCK

Foam paper flowers are a simple, no-fuss way to add a pretty accent to a plain-Jane wall clock. In just minutes you can create dozens of DIY flowers to cover the frame of your clock.

Supplies

scissors

ruler

8 foam paper 9 x 6-inch sheets
   (1 sheet = 2 flowers)

hot glue gun and glue

wall clock

Steps

1. Measure and cut foam sheets into 4 x 4-inch squares.
   (A 9-inch clock will need about 16 squares, which
   will make 16 roses.)

2. Cut each square into a scalloped spiral.

3. Starting from the outside, roll the sheet of foam
   inward to construct a rose. Put a dab of glue at the
   end of the roll to hold the rose in its shape.

4. Once you have assembled enough roses to cover the
   frame of the clock, begin applying a dab of hot glue
   to the bottom of each rose. Stick each onto clock
   and repeat until the frame is full.

Read More

Bolte, Mari. *Fab Fashions You Can Make and Wear.* Sleepover Girls Crafts. North Mankato, Minn.: Capstone Young Readers, 2015.

Fields, Stella. *Accessory Projects for a Lazy Crafternoon.* Lazy Crafternoon. North Mankato, Minn.: Capstone Press, 2016.

Smith, Tana. *DIY Bedroom Decor: 50 Awesome Ideas for Your Room.* Avon, Mass.: Adams Media, 2015.

Internet Sites

Use FactHound to find Internet sites related to this book.

Visit www.facthound.com

Just type in 9781515740094 and go!

About the Author

Heather Wutschke's passion is making her world beautiful — whether that's by designing children's books, painting with her daughter, or completing DIY projects to prettify her house. She believes that good design can improve moods and solve problems. Heather has a degree in graphic design and has spent her career in advertising and publishing. She lives in Missoula, Montana, with her husband and their daughter, Raini. When she isn't staying up late working, she's outside, surrounded by fresh air, mountains, and Montana's big sky.